The Tearing Apart

Luisa Elena Kolker

9/1/2020

To the Students of
Southwestern College~
May you enjoy &
be nourished by these
poems

~Luisa Elena Kolker

D1533849

Copyright © Luisa Elena Kolker, 2020

Cover photograph and design © Luisa Elena Kolker 2020

Author's photograph by Kirana Stover © 2020

All rights reserved. No part of this book may be reproduced in any form, by any means, electronic or mechanical, without permission in writing from the author, except for brief quotations for the purpose of reviews.

The following poems were published in Gargoyle Magazine no. 68 (2018):

Artemis in Taos
D. H. Lawrence Memorial
White Shell Woman
The Tearing Apart

Renegade Oracle Press

Santa Fe, New Mexico, USA
Ibiza, Spain

For those who have traveled a long way and are tired. I extend my hand.

Table of Contents

Waterfalls in the Desert

We drove north to Taos
in the late afternoon heat of mid-July.
Your voice was dry-mute, raspy,
your eyes wild,
a man drowning
in an ancient storm.

As a child you were left alone in the desert
while other children were called home for supper.

You wandered in cast-off clothes,
climbing mountains of dust and coal.
The darkness was your playground.

Not a single drop of care.
Not a single drop.

Only ancestral ash, alcohol, violent survival.
Drought was the forecast in your family
for weeks, months, lifetimes.

We drove past the casino, past the thirsty men
at the twenty-four-hour liquor store,
the baseball-capped tourists at Camel Rock,
all searching for an oasis in the desert.

Not a single drop of care.
Not a single drop.

At Embudo the road was twisted and narrow
pushing the edge of the canyon,
riding the curve of the river
where red willows perished on the banks.

Calcified waterlines on boulders midstream

told the story of ongoing evaporation.

Thunder
jolted our car awake,
like the sound of furniture dragged across an
empty room.
Lightning slashed through black clouds.
Rain slapped the windshield. It insisted,
demanded engagement,
hitting, pounding
our vehicle.

Still your gaze was grim,
your hands rigid at the wheel
as we continued northward.

Any voice, even a scream,
would be lost in that deluge.

Water surged in the river,
seizing territory,
it poured down cliffs and jagged turrets
cascading onto asphalt.

"Look! Waterfalls in the desert!" I said,

because this felt like a gift, a possible
resurrection of all that had
been dry. But, you were long gone.

Not a single drop of care.
Not a single drop.

I watched as new pathways
emerged from high, fortressed spires,
as rock formations
disintegrated in the downpour.

I gave thanks for the miracle that moves,
revises, and allows us
to change.

I give thanks for waterfalls in the desert,
liberating, flowing, unfurling.

Artemis in Taos

Artemis
Artemisia
Artemisia tridentata,
three-pointed leaves
of big sage
that purify, protect,
and heal.

I look like a jogger,
in shorts and a T-shirt,
but I am running, fleeing
like an injured animal
on the dusty roads
of Taos.

I stop to breathe
and cry
in front of Taos Mountain.
I press my face
into the scrubby artemisia,
one of millions
that shelter the desert floor,
and I breathe a prayer.

Goddess Artemisia:
Hunt down my broken
heart.
Please don't kill it.
Bring it back
to me.

D. H. Lawrence Memorial

Frieda condemned your ashes
to a cheerless concrete slab
for all eternity.

As an afterthought,
she adorned your tomb
with a sunflower and a phoenix
to lift you up.

This confusion we call love.

Theft

Petty theft is the rustling of cattle,
the erasing of numbers on a blue-lined ledger,
the last caramel secreted away from its
pleated paper nest.

Theft is the defiling of precious earth
and the slaughter of innocents.

But it's the trifling thefts
I remember best.

The thieves' faces,
the cadence of their voices,
disembodied ghosts
of people I once loved.

Athena Reclines

She is tired.

Living the warrior life is exhilarating for a while.
Being the reformer and rescuer
has its rewards;
pleasure and play
are not among them.

The helmet still gleams. It has a dim appeal.
But the stronger the breastplate,
the sadder the heart.

Athena meets with Aphrodite.

Aphrodite's scent, her touch, her glow,
melt Athena's armor.

Athena surrenders her shield, and it falls
with a clang to the floor.

She strips down to a gossamer slip,
its silk draped in an "X" across her chest.

"Right here," Athena whispers.

Aphrodite presses her hands on Athena's shoulders,
gently blows moist sea-breath into her embattled breast.

Sighing
a long-cloistered exhale,
Athena reclines.

Fear of Masks

I want to claw away
the mask
that stole
your human face.

Sadness, vitriol,
a maelstrom of grief—
any of these would be
less devastating
than your disappearance.

My fear of masks is simple:
What if I move to kiss your face
and you're gone?

You may think I am crazy,
but my kind of fear
is essential
to the survival of love.

Return the mask
to the land of the dead
and come home to me.

Death of a Chair

My parents brought it
from Mexico City to
our living room
in 1964.

It was a throne,
regal, high-backed,
with honey-colored arms
where a king could rest his hands.

As I moved it
from one house to
the next, it
slowly lost its
sheen.

Now it's a skeleton in my garden.

The seasons have corroded
the leather seat,
the frame has faded into gray,
upholstery tacks detached
from their once-anchored depths.

The kings in my world have come and gone.
The chair has remained empty.

On this clear winter day
I will break it into pieces and
throw them into a fierce, dancing fire.

I will warm myself by the flames.

Wild Yellow Orchid

Sturdy green grasses
growing on the banks
like fountains of joy.

A May morning.
Finally there was sunshine,
after months of somber gray.

We walked in the
shade of cottonwoods
so generous and green
even in early spring.

At the edge of pristine water,
three yellow blossoms swayed,
bright and glorious.

A sign of rebirth?

I took their presence personally,
as if they had not appeared
until I needed to see them.

I thought a thing so innocent, so hopeful,
must be protected.

You chuckled and lunged
and in an instant
you plucked one,
pushed it under the band of your hat,
and moved on.

Snowflakes As Big As Your Hand

Dreams are splendid beasts.

The dream gods choose details
my linear mind judges as
inaccurate,
embarrassing,
so delicate is my vanity.

But a few times
my dreams have given to me
new breath and new life.

When I was five,
I dreamt of a perfect red apple
placed in the palms of my hands,
and a pair of pink satin toe shoes
carefully fitted onto my feet
by a woman who loved me.

When I awoke,
delighted beyond reason,
I could still feel the shoes' silken weight,
the cool roundness of the apple.

Half a century later
that apple,
those shimmering toe shoes,
still mine,
make my heart
smile.

Yesterday,
if I were the weeping kind,
I would have cried myself to sleep.

Instead I dreamt of snow.

Standing before an enormous window,
I watched
as snowflakes
the size of my hand
gentled down through
the shimmering winter air,

their designs so extravagant
I could see
the intricate grace
of each one.

Fuel for another fifty years.

Black Hat

Rage is the disowned child
of grief
and terror.

It deadens all
that desires
connection or hope,
leaving orphans
under its battered sun.

Removes the humanity
from the tenderness of
possibility.

Decimates what grows,
scorches earth
till a solitary tree
raises its arms in surrender.

Hang your black hat
on a wounded, charred branch.

You will be safe now
as nothing here
will ever grow.

The Tooth

It cracked in half
when she was ten.
A failed jungle gym
handstand.

A grown-up said:
You have ruined
your looks
forever."

The tooth was feral and
broken,
a pointed
dagger
to dig her way
out of
suffocating
rubble,

a menacing, wild knife
to threaten enemies
with death
or devouring.

Demons

When we met,
your demons
slept
in a primitive
part of your brain,
exiled there
in boyhood
as your father held you
hostage
on his aroused lap.

Love made you
careless.
The demons
burst through the newly
unlocked
door.

They set fire
to all you held dear.

Your liver-damaged father long dead,
he doesn't hold you prisoner
but the demons do.

When you remember
to close the door,
all is silent.

But through the cracks
seep
black smoke
and the smell
of a dying animal.

White Shell Woman

Ojo Caliente Hot Springs, New Mexico

Wanderers in need of new life,
in need of water,
have always sought
the springs that rise
out of dry earth.

White Shell Woman,
White Shell Woman,
I need your help
to heal my heart.

White Shell Woman,
White Shell Woman,
I am drowning
in empty spaces.
I need your help.

She is well known
to the Zunis, the Navajo,
and all the ancient ones.

Years ago,
I heard her name
from my friend Steven,
who said she lived
at the sacred springs
of Ojo Caliente.

On my fifty-seventh birthday
I need to visit her,
so I drive northward
to her sanctuary.

White Shell Woman,
White Shell Woman,
I speak to you
and instantly you
appear.

You show me a pure
white shell
embedded
in the cliff
beside the spring,

a tiny shell,
empty for so long,
exposed to the
parching heat of time.

White Shell Woman,
White Shell Woman,
I offer you my old shell.

What can you do
with this brittle
bowl that once was
filled with life
at the bottom of
this desert ocean?

White Shell Woman,
White Shell Woman,
you hold me and
offer me refuge
in your amniotic rhythm.

White Shell Woman,
White Shell Woman,
I feel you loosen the
dying life that clings
to my shell.

And now you speak to me:

Old shells become
new homes,
you say.

Old shells become
new homes.

A Passage Through Spain

If you want to make me weep,
speak to me of Spain.

I know the darkness there.
The bodies buried under
cobblestone streets,
the tyranny of kings
and church
and a dictator who ruled
for almost forty
years.

And I know there
was once a paradise
where souls of all
faiths inhaled the
elixir of fresh-baked
bread, saffron-infused
sweets, and rose water.

In Granada's candlelit caves
gypsy dancers spark
lightning bolts
that make your heart ache
for that which cannot be named.

If you want to make me weep,
speak to me of Spain.

The last Moorish king of Andalucía
looked back upon his majestic Alhambra
and sighed for what had been.

I, too, remember
the magical, arabesque palaces
of my youth,
the beauty of wild, flowing waters,
held in my hands.

What I remember
about Spain
is that I was young and
the world was a garden
that grew me.

The moment of budding was brief.

I cradle it in the tips of my fingers;
inhale
its evanescent
perfume.

Grief

She waits in the rented flat
that is precisely as you left it
many years ago:
faded black-and-white
fleur-de-lis wallpaper,
blue ticking on the
pillowcases.

She bides her time,
sits by a sealed window
that drips tears of condensation
as the heat inside
meets the cold outside.

She knits one, perls two,
knits one, perls two,
like Madame Defarge
patiently awaiting the revolution.

She is like your grandmother,
recalling
details of her childhood
with vivid clarity
even as her body ages.

One day, when you have not
prepared for stormy weather,
you discover
a skeleton key
in your pocket.

To avoid the downpour,
you use it to
unlock a door
and walk into
the steamy room

where she wears a faded
bathrobe and
shuffles
her canasta cards.

Slap, slap, slap, go the cards.

"Welcome back," she says.
"I've been
waiting for you."

The Servant

Never forget Ninshubur,
the servant
holding vigil
on the surface of the Earth,

keening and wailing for her mistress,
Queen Inanna,
who is
lost in the depths
of soul darkness,
gone below, beyond the
seven gates,
into the Underworld.

Ninshubur beats fiercely
on the drum of sorrow,
throws back her head,
screams scalded-flesh sounds
of mourning,
summoning the intervention
of gods and ministers.

Inanna is draped in lapis,
with kohl-rimmed sultry eyes.

For thousands of years it has been she
on the marquee.

But remember, Inanna:

Without the servant
who saved your royal ass,
you would still be
rotting
like bad meat
on a hook
in the Underworld.

The Desert of Liberation

Desert dwellers recognize each other.
They know the secret communion
of parched earth and dusty shoes.

The lush commotion of verdant places
pales in comparison to the nourishment
of kinship in the desert.

Surviving the death of
what you once considered real,
you will blossom

like a mysterious flower
that opens once
every hundred years.

The Tearing Apart

Before life can begin
there is the tearing apart.

There are graceful,
romantic ways
to describe
birth,
but the truth is
it is a ripping apart
of union,
and there is blood
where there once
had been fusion.

Persephone,
perfectly
merged with
Demeter,
is torn apart
from the world
she knew,
blood-red
poppies
still
clutched in her
milk-soft hands.

She is abducted
into the
Underworld,
which is
sometimes
the only way
you can leave home.

Harvest

When it's time
you'll have to leave the party.

Though your champagne
still fizzes in the goblet,
and cherries beckon on the branch.

Though graceful snowflakes
drape the foothills with
a wondrous cloak;
though you haven't written
the last line
of your

poem.

When it's time
you'll have to leave the party.

Some won't notice
you've left the room.
Some may be relieved.
Some will walk with you
to the door,
stroking your hand, kissing your
face, telling you how much
they love you.

When you cross the threshold,
may it be
with a flurry of love,
a festival of wildflowers,
a full glass of wine

when it's time to leave the party.

Wave Goodbye

To escape to another galaxy

travel lightly

leave what weighs you down

break free of the Earth's gravitational
pull.

Stop making excuses

for why
you don't
really

live your life.

First Rain

For Daniel

Four months old,
eyes the color of the blue-green
Mediterranean.

You are so new
to this world.

A gray spring day,
storm clouds
racing in from the north
of the island.

Our rattly blue car
bumping along
washboard ridges
on the Spanish
red dirt road.

On either side of us,
the fruits of paradise:
fig, almond, olive,
carob, orange.

Tires splashing
puddles
reflecting a cottony
sky.

I pull over;
streams roll down
the windshield.

The sound of your
in-breath,
a question-concern-delight:
"Ah! Oh!"

I lean to lift you,
perch you on my hip;
we walk into the orchard.

A fig tree
is our umbrella.

Slowly, reverently,
you lift your face,

eyelashes fluttering
into the
mysterious.

Winter on a Spanish Island

Ibiza, Spain

I am cold
sitting on the restaurant terrace
overlooking the sea.
But I don't care.
I came here
for healing
not for the intoxicating swelter of summer.

I came here
to retrieve
the soul of
my younger self,
who left on an August afternoon,
infant in her arms,
obeying love and obligation—
her dying father on another
continent.

No idea
she would not
return
for twenty-five years.

I remember
the comfort
of my innocence
before life
said:

Sorry, but we have other plans.

Strange Tears

We are much older
than we were
not so long ago.

Yesterday we were
planting bulbs
for spring.

Today we
gather roses
dried
on the stem.

Tanit's Cave

Cala San Vicente, Ibiza, Spain

The ancient Phoenician
path is steep,
undulates like a serpent,
makes
muscles burn

I arrive and see
rusted iron bars
blocking the
sacred shrine

like a cage
or a prison.

The goddess
doesn't live here
anymore,
I speak aloud

Descending
to the valley
I walk
hot footsteps

each one
sending my fire
into the
receiving
earth

each step
enumerating
violation
incarceration
of the
feminine

Where is my path,
I ask

In the feather soft
branches of
pitiusa pines

an arc
of light,

luminous
threads of
love,

shines on
the winding walkway

leading me
back to
the sea

A Prayer for Marta

Ibiza, Spain

On the stretch of road
between Santa Eulália and San Carlos,
I think of the two of you.

Bodies melding into one,
flying free,
on his motorcycle.

Your arms wrapped
around him,
his warm, sturdy back
protecting your heart.
You were finally
happy—

at last a reason
to be here,
a reason
to believe in love.

I see the two of you
just as the road
curves,
before the car's headlights
blind you.

Slow-motion keeling
sideways in darkness,
sparks of light as
metal meets wet asphalt,

softness scraping
cool, hard ground.

He died. You survived.

But you have not
returned.

I want to bring you home.

My Mom at 92

On the autumn full moon
your little dog
snuffles your face
to wake you

You pat her
nose
and
rise,
feet touching
the chenille
rug

Your legs won't
hold you,
you arc into
a free fall

The floor
is smooth,
cold

horizontality
offers
a new perspective

Eye to eye
with baffled
Carlota,
who licks
your face and
climbs
on board
for this
new ride.

Second Saturn Return

I wrote their names on pieces
of lined notebook paper—
the bad actors
I hired to be the

monster
hero
narcissist
sex god
deviant
vandal
bad boy

in my
real-life
movie.

I crushed their names
in my hand,
threw the schoolbook paper
on the fire.

"Goodbye."
"No more."
"Done forever."

Never again.

How quickly
the flames clawed and
consumed them.

How beautiful to watch
dead white paper
bursting into ash.

The Black Madonna of Montserrat

Lady of the Fertile Darkness,
Lady of the Mountain,
the orb of the world
is weightless
in your hands.

The child of the universe,
placid and serene,
rests on your knee.

I walk solemnly
toward you
inside your golden chapel.
Your hollow gaze
dissolves me,
revealing light
inside my emptiness.

Outside your basilica,
the jagged peaks
of the Montserrat mountains
are an electrocardiogram
of the human heart,
spiking in distress,
quivering in fibrillation.

La Moreneta,
can you heal
this dying world?

Me, Too

On the old shows
in the Golden Age
of Television,
the magician's
beautiful assistant
strikes a pose
in her
sequined
sheath.

She has consented
to lie in the
coffin-shaped box
that is like
Goldilocks'
first
ill-fitting
bed.

Head popping out,
feet exposed,
the rest of her
has
been
disappeared.

She is an obedient
lady of the era,
grinning
as the dapper man,
in impeccable
coat, tails, and
top hat,

saws her in half.

She is split
in two.
And still
she smiles.

Bad Housekeeping

I just noticed
the cobwebs
on the passenger side
of my bed,

a feral net of arachnid-woven
gauze
between
the windowsill and
that
long
unused
bedside
table.

Grow,
little spiders!
Breed!
Catch your
feast with
ease.

I give you permission to
dine upon
all
intruders.

Precious Nectar

For Mara

A dusting of snow and ice
in late spring.

White cherry blossoms
burned brown.

Their sweetness short-lived,
never to fruit.

Your mother
grew, blossomed, and birthed you,

precious nectar.

She left us on a dove-wing day.

Viral Encephalitis

Inside the winter chrysalis
my existence was
an empty, unlit room.

I could not feel
my feet,
could not
taste or smell.

I saw only
the dim veil
between
the worlds,

a silky-mesh
nightmare where
no sunlight
could warm me.

Stretch.
Unfurl.
I commanded myself,
but my voice
had no sound.

Help me.
I am alone in here.
I am dying.

But my friends
outside
could not hear.

Six different doctors said:
You're just nervous.
Take an Ativan.

Finally, in the spring
the neurologist gave the
diagnosis.

Now in late summer
the chill of winter
remains.

In the garden today
I watched a black butterfly
with gold-rimmed wings.

She alighted on a wavering
stalk of mullein,
sipping fragrant
yellow flowers,

and then wobbled
from rue to rosemary,
penstemon to sage.

From bitter to sweet,
sweet to bitter.

Black butterfly
summer.

The Day Before Leaving

High-desert winter junipers
blue green black
in the harsh angled sun

My other home is by the sea,
a continent far away

Some places and people will never be able
to reside side-by-side
though long days of travel
may bridge us
for a while

I fear my solitude is a good loneliness
No ruin of dignity, no shattering of trust
and that I will stay here

My intimacies are with land,

mountains that roll and reflect
the moods of each moment,

ocean waters that speak in colors
turquoise, indigo, silky gray

This earth will not betray you.

I Dream of Eating Watermelon

I'm in the backyard at my childhood home
on Leland Street.

Dad, Granny, and the aunts
are eating watermelon on a
midsummer evening
as the sun is dimming.

In the realm of my ancestors
it is always summer.

I hear the timeless cadence
of the locusts and smell the
sweet-rotten flowering
of the towering tulip tree.

Dad smiles.

"We'll be waiting for you," he says.

"Soon," I ask, "or not for a while?"

"Yes," he says.

I apologize for not visiting
more often.

"We're here," he says, soundlessly.

I am young and old
on that eternal summer night.

I will be there again soon,
but not for a little while.

Acknowledgments

I am grateful to those who held me close during my Black Butterfly year—especially Adam Kolker, Jason Kolker, Ann Filemyr, Onde Chymes, Daniel Kolker-Murphy and Mara Lafferty. Melissa Chianta, thank you for your astute editing skills and psychic literary abilities. Thank you to my mother Marielena Zelaya Kolker who read poems, plays, and stories to me when I was little. Michael S. Glaser, you were my first poetry teacher; I have never forgotten how you introduced me to the secret life of words.

Made in the USA
Columbia, SC
20 July 2020

14294319R00050